Tales from the Other Box

Rick Dove

Burning Eye

This edition published by Burning Eye Books 2020

www.burningeye.co.uk

@burningeyebooks

Burning Eye Books
15 West Hill, Portishead, BS20 6LG

ISBN 978-1-911570-89-9

Rick Dove is a London-based poet and storyteller. Born in Tooting and raised in south London in the 1980s and 1990s, Rick has witnessed the effects of both increasing multiculturalism and, more recently, gentrification on the same childhood streets, and, as such, his work reflects on both societal and personal change and how these two forces interact as we grow.

A regular on London's burgeoning poetry scene since late 2015, Rick's performance features have included the Boomerang Club; Spoken Word London; Speak=; the ClitArt Festival 2017; Crystal Palace International Festival; Once Upon a Mic; The Chocolate Poetry Club, including a residency in 2016; Cabinet Office GDS Black History Month Exhibition 2017, and touring with the Errant Stage for the Big Red Poetry Tour Wandsworth Arts Fringe 2018 and 2019. As a poetry slam participant Rick has come second in the UK Slam Final 2019, been a highly commended semi-finalist of the BBC Edinburgh Fringe Slam 2018, he won the Farrago Slam (November 2018), and won the Hammer & Tongue Hackney's 2018/2019 season.

Rick's work has been published widely, including pieces in *London South Bank University Anthology, London Spoken Word Anthology, New Poetry Magazine, Soapbox, Guardian Online* and *the Morning Star*. His first solo pamphlet, *Haigha's Noosphere Canticles*, was published by William Cornelius Harris Publishing in 2017. This is Rick's first full published collection of poetry

Tales from the Other Box

*To my African Queen, my Danish Prince,
and the Little Boy pointing at the Emperor*

CONTENTS

FIRST WORDS

for years   you bite your tongue
moderate your rage   play dumb
pretend   you don't hear what they say
maintain   a dignified silence
stay quiet in the face of snarling
with your boiling blood
one drop polluted
with fight and flight
where neither is appropriate
this is an office job   not a pub
so you bite your tongue

you ignore the patronising tones
even though your education
(both street and academic)
means that you know better than they assume
and they assume   they know better than you
you maintain   a dignified silence
allow them to explain   how your personal experience
is wrong   is far-fetched
and there is familiarity   to their contempt

you pretend   that shop floor security
aren't playing chaperone   as you browse
you keep your head down   as not to arouse
suspicions already evident
you touch nothing   because evidence
you keep calm   while explaining
(for the thousandth time that day)
why it isn't okay   to profile in this way
it is a heated exchange   and you know why
but play dumb when asked to explain
you bite your tongue
this is not the hill to die on

you respond politely to where are you from
again and again   explain the region
then the city   then the town   then the street
then the maternity ward
reductio ad absurdum   (getting bored)
so you go the other way
explain the country and continent
the planet   our interstellar neighbourhood
the galaxy of possibilities they refuse to see
you are never from where they need you to be
and there is familiarity to their contempt
so you bite your tongue

you listen to others explain how you don't belong
in the land that you were born   the only one
that ever kept you warm
you keep smiling (a little lopsided now)
your tongue is swollen   heavy from all the biting
you smile   but not with busy teeth
not like the cartoons   not like the Jim Crow ones
you don't dance anymore   for fear of compliments
you bite your tongue
you bite your tongue
you bite your tongue
remembering what your parents said once

it is not your job to hold the lantern
to show others out of the dark

until suddenly one day
you wake at a ripe old age
realising the lantern was never for them
or to light their way
it was yours alone
a reminder of the sun
there is familiarity to their contempt
but there is fight and flight upon your tongue

PROUD FLESH

the hardest lessons of history repeating
repeat themselves even after being
even after being implicitly understood
the first time
like *Empire is a hate crime*
(even after being)
like portmanteau is a skin tone abstract
as the scars that a whip makes
as skin breaks
can be proud flesh
can be preowned
remains
the hardest lessons of history repeating
repeat themselves
and every one a teacher

THE MATCH COLLECTOR

in those months after   he was Hansel in reverse
picking up skimming stones from the edges of clichés
by limpid pools so far from home
where the lotus grows   the dragons roam
these uncharted zones he would return to
stooping in reflection for collecting thoughts
and pieces of soul he once dropped
returning   to gathering himself
stopped and singing in the bell jar
resonating with ricochets
a specimen held in stillborn ripples
nestled as memories
undeveloped rolls of sepia kisses
a portrait montage of where he was once
matchbooks of where he was once

in the hollow multicoloured patches
woven together   taken together
his *out of the woods* is swallowed
stilled with the sounds of trees falling
boughs breaking as lullabies should

in the months after   he was always wandering home
finding his way on the scent of sulphur
on the soon to be glowing embers
of flashes to ashes   a lust for dust
and cold earth he could bury himself under
clicking locked tumblers and whiskey rocks
in peaty deeps sticky   he was keeping stock
under glass fearing the future   leaving each box
unopened   each book
unread
in the hope that one day   once again
they might lead him home

GLACIAL

you never forget your first

it is damp trudge from the car
across the bright bustle of main road
from the side street past hostel and minimart
from way back in our class
the other side of society
the long way around our tears in puddles
so profound now   so pronounced
and finally out of the dark
on this of all days
a long way from our late arrivers' spot
today   you are chatting
we are moving in memories
slower than i remember
me talking about the weather
linking it to his pneumonia
it was AIDS-related   you say
so nonchalantly
numbed by the practices of having said it on repeat
a thousand times in our recent history
and once too many
you sound empty   so detached
like if you treat it like small talk
we might shrink it   into something
inconsequential
but this makes it impossible to see
as it whistles into me
a singing bomb bouncing
it is raining

you never forget your first

it is damp trudge   arm in arm from the car
out of the dark
the long way around
these puddles of being   that prejudices make

in the bright bustle of mainstream from the side-lines
wet feet sticky from wading the hostilities
still falling   still settling
and i am not crying
lest they see me   call it *girly*
and the only thing i will remember of today
is how feelings can park themselves
in the *late arrivers'* spot of your gut
and still be making their way to your brain
days   and weeks   and years later
like mourning is metastases creeping
and it is raining

you never forget your first

it is a forever damp trudge to a memorial
where some of us are mourners
in amongst the bright bustle
of mainstream and high street
he never liked poetry   you say
so i write this eventually   years later
from these indelible memories
in the bustle   of finally being mainstream
where some of us are mourners
still

you never forget your first

it was raining
no one wore black
in accordance with wishes
and the candles we lit
made rainbows

TREADING WATER

Plasticity
a special property
of various materials
allowing them
to deform
irreversibly
without breaking

trauma has plasticity
and we are all single-use
longevity in toxicity
forever leeching through our adhesions
a desire for permanence
when thrown away

VISIT

finally   i meet your gaze
that burdened one   eyes carrying questions
teaspoons in the tray   trembling
a rattle for all those baby steps
a warning there are snakes   hiding here in the asking
in the stirring   in your gaze
the all too familiar one   made of pity and piety
with all the jokes about a dropped *e*
stripped away   inappropriate   caught
my eyes   like saucers are blanched raw
widened white and scarlet patina
with all the wonder stripped back
to fresh and naked   like the day that i was born
smooth and slippy   a squall   salty to taste
still spilling warm   falling debris
you sheltered from once   molten flecks of sky
falling
like the chicken said *the sky is falling*
i was your sky once

your gaze   stewing steep
the silence repeats every inquiry
as if the echoes themselves
see all the journeys   now upon skin
where my dreams have taken me
how my dreams make me   breath
heavy   wet and wild
constantly whispering underneath

finally   i meet your gaze
a freshly made stranger
kept away   just long enough to forget
as if love could ever be   unremembered
i was your sky once   until the rain

fine   i say
you say nothing   and pour the tea

LESSONS ON FOLDED TIME

you taught me about assumptions
and today in your fortune cookie

love is a present
that you can give
every day that you live

and so here
(showing my workings)
are some underlying assumptions

you will never forget a face
and every face   will be verbatim made   of familiar shapes

and you will learn   all there is to know about these shapes
and that knowledge   will never fade

you will have an eidetic memory
especially for these shapes

your mind will make photographs of everything
these will never sepia with nostalgia

you will remain

your eyesight will be perfect until the day you die

your hindsight will not be blinded by the light of trauma

you will always be greeted by smiling faces

have no fear
you will always leave a place
better and brighter than it was
before you arrived

you will learn how the shapes (that make faces) can change

and you will always recognise these changes

you will leave this place   like every place safe
and you will always know
that this will be the case

every day of your life   will be the same until the day you die

you will recognise the shapes
and every interaction that you have
will be (in some way) familiar
and you will always get better

you will always get better at remembering faces
and you will miss nothing
especially not yourself

you will never arrive
at a surprise party
without a gift

you will always get better

you will remain

you can always get better

love is a present
that you can give
every day that you live

assumes that you will always want to
assumes that you will always be able to

it is today again
as your fortune cookie
taught me this

SAMARITAN

we don't use that word
we never use that word

it is out of the blue
and the black glass
is not a mirror anymore
wreathed in static halo
tomb of the unknown number
starting with familiar area code
i know and i know

in my hand
there is a trembling voice held close
that forgoes no pleasantries
but is not pleasant
there is a crack
the black glass is not a mirror anymore
i can see tears on the pane
racing down a cheek
and i know

we don't use that word
we never use that word

in my hand my chest aches
my heart races
there is a crack
it is out of the blue
an unknown number of times
this has happened
to soldier through
we dare not count
anything but reasons
each of my fingers triggers twitching
stay for the kids
chaste for the kids
for their wellbeing

because London rent is expensive
because this is not the worst of it
i wish that i had more to give
that i was allowed to exist
there is a crack
in my voice
as i say this
as she acknowledges
at least this way
i will always be around to listen

to keep us safe
to save me
she won't use that word
we never use that word
because we know
in the right light
black glass is always a mirror

PLAYING RED ROVER

alien
is instructive
as some people never acknowledge
Curiosity[1] is invasive

---

1 Curiosity is the name of the NASA's Mars rover that made planetfall/
invasion 6th August 2012

YOUR YAW YORE

there is a time before names
in certain parts of our history
over the sea from West Africa
and so   by extension
through enough of black diaspora
(whether slave trade migrated or not)
in certain parts of our culture
there is a time before names

it is our tradition
born in the harsh reality
of infant mortality
a superstition
that death couldn't find you
as a baby
if you didn't have a name

so in certain parts of our history
a time before names
remains

in the free paper
on the news ticker
on the webpage
it is Wednesday afternoon
as *black teenager* dies again

THE CHAT

i heard it first at seven   the day they called me *gollywog*
and as the word passed these lips   to meet Mum's ear
a tear   and every time since then   i am back there
little boy lost there   wondering when i will grow up
praying and praying (like that was ever enough)
that the world will too   strange then that this was too
my childhood's end   there in an eighties living room
as Mum   and Dad   and i   had **The Chat**

and my dad tells the tale   regales again and again
in his final days   about his early years on this isle
how *only black in the village* was actually a thing
and how it was him   and how on summer's day
at no more than eight   a policeman at the gate
came to tell his mum he couldn't go to the corner shop
alone again   he hadn't stolen anything
but the shopkeeper (like so many back then)
was not one for details   except that simple   single one
that still holds us back   and later that evening
Granny and Grandad gave my eight-year-old dad **The Chat**

and i rehearse it with a girlfriend   the same night
of our first tiff   late on a date about twenty-oh-three
(the year   not the hour) as she suggests we hail a cab
and her privilege hits me there   hits me square
hits me full force in the derriere   *i won't be able to flag one here*
i SNAP snarky   implying *maybe it should be you*
wading the flooded gutter in your good shoes...
and later that evening   as i am cleaning her boots
she and i have **The Chat**

and this is how it has been for generations
parents to their children   star-crossed lovers in
        explanation
in conversation after conversation   spelling out
how being black (though having some advantages)

will get you treated as lesser by some
make you a target to some
put you in the crosshairs of some
and this is something a quartet of
Carl Lewis Linford Christie Usain Bolt and Jesse Owens can't
    outrun
it is a baton we're still passing   and this is me to you my son
for that is how i will have to give it to my boy   saying
i hope the world will grow   so you never truly know
this feeling of being so conspicuous   and yet so small
of representing an entire skin tone   on your own   alone
because i know whenever you feel the weight of that
it will crush you   flat
and you deserve to be on show
only when you choose to be
and now you are fully grown
and in possession of our truth
i know you will guard it well   until it is due
but i hope and pray (like that has ever been enough)
that it ends with you
and hopefully one day
a black man merely putting pen to page
will stop being a political act
but until then we have *The Chat*

DEBUT

shuffle on
she haunts the vestibule
pigeon steps
timing her patter for pity
on tiny feet
a moment after we have our seats
falls still
before the doors close
beholds the stage
moved as she speaks
small voice
racing to finish before the train reaches full speed
before its full-throated rushing
drowns out her soliloquy

and we
are held
an audience captive in silences of habit
a cold light spot oppressively complicit
bright inoperative theatre
replete with critics
bile and spleen
sterile incredulity
when she finishes
soul spilled like milk
there are no tears
there is scant applause
barely acknowledgment at all
for we all know there is more to her story
some will give her pennies for their thoughts
hoping they will return to silence
while others   skip this track entirely

FAMILIAR

in darkened streets
where logically this
conspiracy in complexion
should help hide me
i *stand out* (apparently)
enough   it seems
to call the police
for questioning
for interrogating memories
to be pushed past
to be manhandled
squashed and trodden down

the following morning
during the rush hour commute
magically invisible again
as *the help* should be

CHRYSALIS (AFTER ZHUANGZI)

Once upon a time   i dreamt i was a rich man
profiting carefree   hither and thither   paying no
taxes   and no heed to the rules that hindered others
explaining feminism to my daughters   pregnancy to
mothers   to all intents and purposes a rich man   i was
conscious only of my happiness as a rich man   totally
unaware that i was myself   Soon i awaked and there i
was   veritably myself again   Now i do not know whether
i was then a creole dreaming that i was a rich man   or
whether i am now a rich man   dreaming i have a soul

LIFTING THE LID

i always felt that Schrödinger's cat was black
so damned familiar   to be that
experiment of the white man
to be put in a box
to be both alive and dead and theoretical
for the sake of someone else's critical thinking
for someone else's education
just an impossible image
inside someone else's head
subjected   subjugated   sold and bred
and made undead
by this our shared history
that neglects to mention
how the torture and murder of small animals
is one of the early warning signs of psychopathy
but you know this already
and i know this intimately
having an affinity with that moggy
frequently while out jogging
doing laps at dawn and watching others' scorn
as they cross themselves and cross the street
to keep away from me
to keep me from crossing their path

and you may laugh
but i always felt that Schrödinger's cat was black
so damned familiar that
feeling of being (or not being) at the whims of fate
the superpositions and quantum states
of being a number one (for weeks) sexual fantasy
and the lynch mob scapegoat simultaneously
this eternal duality of the word *hung*
about being corrected once
by an old white man to say *hanged*
as if by way of reparations or apology
he should improve my grammar and silence me
subtly put a lid on me and bottle me

to store me away in the cool and dark place
as if being seen (and heard) might change me
and make me real
instead of this velveteen victim
of the *white man's burden*
that he'd now rather forget
and stuff into a box with poison pill
to be dispatched
to be euphemistically   lost

and so like Schrödinger's cat
i am both fully assembled and flat packed
numbered irrationally   the root of two worlds
some insist are mutually exclusive
Black   &   British
two worlds squished and sealed into this
to be or not to be
by these imperial measurements
in these ghetto experiments
to be or not to be
poisoned by this maddening society
that both co-opted and rejected me
adopted and neglected me
that still imagines me
taking jobs while stealing welfare simultaneously
and continuously   puts me in a box
and then ends up hating that box
when it comes to define me
and leaves it feeling all the GUILTY of its acts
recalling its history   our shared history
founded on all the murders we would rather not see
early warning signs of psychopathy that
the mutability of facts

so you see
i always felt that Schrödinger's Cat was black
so damned familiar to me was his story
this duality of being (and not being)
forever at the mercy

of those out there doing the seeing
and their own curiosities
and PLEASE don't get me started
on my bisexuality

FUMBLING

at this time   tie signs of couples   snuggled smugly
together   teeter on possessive in heteronormative
fingers twitching the strings of marionettes
dancing   furtive advancing   glancing
askance in watching who is watching   they are overly
overtly wrapped enraptured   this is foreplay on display
and only permitted   if you fit
and you will notice it   if you never did

KISSED BY THE LIGHT OF ROBOTS

at the junction
we gave way to everything

stopped still   an eternity
golden and green in the contact

on the corner   dancing sparks
indicating a turn   in their flickering

and it strikes me
i heard them called *robots* once

ON THE BUTTON

when it comes to the time
i am never sure how to approach it
announce it   or pronounce it

does it rhyme with *this*
like a soft slipped kiss
of oft-parted lips

or is it *us*
just us
unique to us
and such touch
a first thrust
so crackling with the thunder and electricity
of a connection complete
that it renders me
but particles and dust

and too much of this
leaves me
in open-mouthed
slack-jawed wonder
awesome struck
or somehow pondering aptly
about how much of this
is below the surface
constantly

for most of it
is below the surface
we know this
that the greater percentage
of all knowledge
is hidden
in the forbidden
in sly denials sidling purblind
in the fumblings serving only to ignite

righteous rumblings
at the depths of it
this aptly shaped
banana skin
tripping in its rippling
the fruit the serpent missed in its offerings
responding to plosives and sibilance

for most of it
is below the surface
sinking all such epic patriarchal engineering
all such commandeering projects
that the boy in me
is still pointing his finger at the damn
still looking for land
and screaming constantly internally
ICEBERG

even as you show me how to place my tongue and lips
and teach me how to breathe
how to say your name
how this word
however we say it
has no taboos left
for the heft of bliss and flames
pressed into flesh is a gift

most of it
is below the surface

you say

REGENT'S CANAL: A SUNDAY

giggling canal-side   we muse
the mumbles stumbled   stub and stumped
toes dipped
struck dumb by this banal whiling trip
of skipped stones
slip some accented foreign tongues
that reminisce the epic tell of it

a gap

makes accidental beauty
amongst the debris of industry
and grips to bind these lines to time
as i watch your lips
in memoriam mime mesmeric
words you dare not say
a gilded water rose
rushing blood flows and lilies
flood the face with gilded feelings

suddenly your hand
and leading questions
to define this enchanting space
abound with water birds calling
beckoning to bathe
dipped in tears of willow
your favourite green
fruit of a divine decision tree
sweet goads me hot into temptation
and delivers me open source philosophy
straining at the start
a game's afoot
once more
unto the breach
once more
to feel your cheek
caress these errant fingers

BUCKET LIST

capitalism is
putting out a fire   with a bucket
with a trickle of a hole at the base of it
and having to carry   said bucket
from the lake edge   to the seat of it
(the fire   that is)
and what is your strategy in this
is it in a steady stream of half buckets
anxiously and hurriedly
backwards and forwards   forwards and backwards
more than enough
to make sure of enough
or is it more conservatively
in believing you have time
to plug the hole   before you go
and committing early   to that belief
that efficiency   and lack of waste
especially of your own energy
is the key

capitalism is
filling the bucket   with poured possessions
to a raging fire   made of need

capitalism is
the bucket makers' greed
selling straw as kindling   with black market weed
there's a hole in my bucket   dear Liza   dear Liza
you used to sing to me
that one bucket was enough for Maslow's hierarchy
you used to sing to me
there's a hole in my bucket   dear Liza
that all abundance is about anxiety
around security
about the fear of fire that our news reels bleed
there's a hole in my bucket
you used to sing to me
my bucket   a hole

capitalism is
black market buckets
reselling buckets to stockpile
to price fix
reading bucket diplomas at bucket universities
studying an amendment to the very definition of freedom
all about buckets   and straw
and a straw man's deeds

capitalism is
a media obsessed with fires
even the ones with deniers
even the ones we started abroad
and still sell straw to feed

capitalism is
the very idea of buckets
with buckets as seeds
and bucket peer reviewed
year-on-year growth in perpetuity
and bucket salesman arsonists
suggesting the blood of refugees
is as good as water
and better for the buckets' longevity
it is only thicker
when you're family   you see

capitalism is
an endless game of buckets
bucketing down with rain
and when into every life   some rain must fall
the bucket is panacea
catch   all

capitalism is
our willing acceptance
and yet total denial
of all this
until we kick it
(the bucket   that is)

READ QUEEN'S GAMBIT

Wicked that little wink you give in whispers
Riposte embossed with trick of tic and trapped
Yearning   that tempts this turning tongue to twister

Double down the ante and all that glitters
On a whim   a stake that through the heart exacts
Wicked that little wink you give in whispers
Every gift of misunderstandings' vistas
Retold   with corruption's ever-growing gap
Yearning that tempts this turning tongue to twister

Lisp   and list this every step that differs
Every turn   and move with new meanings mapped
Wicked that little wink you give in whispers
Daring poetry to be so hot it flickers
Like candle fire like burning desire   racked
Yearning that tempts this turning tongue to twister

Down   and down   the rabbit hole in rivers
Eternal wish to drown   this smiling cat
Wicked that little wink you give in whispers
Yearning that tempts this turning tongue to twist here

NARCISSUS

reflecting
in those moments
spellbinding arousal brings
aware of the reprisals
pheromones will sing
bathed in your panting
drowning in your skin
i am a rifle
repeating
I am
I am
I am

ON META MORPHING

Remnants of failed veiled bigotry declared
Unwashed bards with untrained ears are gristle
Every word a singing bird confessing fears
Digress not   poems must stop   must stand and stare

And be only what we met afore belittled
Remnants of failed veiled bigotry declared
This yardstick white privilege all disgrace and heirs

We hear you hack-hacking with the dog whistle
Every word a singing bird confessing fears

We hear you [insert ref to ivory tower here]
Each speech   each treatise and every epistle
Remnants of failed veiled bigotry declared
End of days if words do not remain rarefied air

But beware   my highborn lord in lyric castle
Every word a singing bird confessing fears
For we know more of moreish and green-eyed cares
Our art carved as darts and launched as missiles
Remnants of failed veiled bigotry to clear
Every word a singing bird freed and rare

D

it is not long after my eighteenth birthday   and we have
gone public   back in private i am aback akimbo taken
and she is riding high on my thigh   bringing
herself to her second orgasm   something i will later learn is
called *tribbing*   and i am being used   i know this   even
here and now   having no frame of reference   and having
no frame of reference   i question if this is normal
knowing full well how we have ended up here
is not   is anything but is nothing of the sort   and she is
bringing herself to her second orgasm   and it is not hot

eighteen plays thirty-four   so my mind is wandering
all the while   to thoughts of what sport could bear such a
score
settling on rugby   via relative sexual peaks
between moans and screaming   and something deep
repressed memories   i will forever keep

thinking Will Carling went to this university
and Nasser Hussain

i am thinking of England
and it will never be the same

MIDDLE ENGLAND CUCKOO

and finally i am realising these plague dreams
that vague be in deeps of me
until i will be Moses in the Windrushes
and Pharaoh will fear me

time passes   striking this alien flyer
with interloping cipher
with all that happened before
falling heavy handed as weighty history
held privately behind closed doors
time moves it to stirring
to longing to shed the plume feathers
it had flocked with and was born into
urges it into wishing not to fly
wishing to be bald and naked as it tries
a new emperor's new cast-offs for size

with all the high talk
of promised lands fading
Pharaoh's men say
i was invading
even as they read my invitation

time strikes the usurper cipher
born out of place and out of line
thrusting into the light
into the white space
safety envisioned at the end of the tunnel
time takes it out of the closet
from the shadows
out of the whirring churning gears of the combine
out to show how this awkward bird
can click clipped
on the tip of a mechanical tongue
it adopted so young
so it might be here
in time
at home

because Pharaoh's men once told me
i wasn't black enough
to complain with the other slaves
i shit you not
like they really and truly believed
blackness has degrees
and is not
just
one
drop

time strikes it
comes to all senses
to these rarefied airs and graces
truth comes into full view
and it will be screaming *CUCKOO*
dreaming *CUCKOO*
emancipated just for you
so you might take note of the time
overdue be amused
by this strange hatchling of a curate's egg
with its tales to tell
begging for a bell
seconds out
for fight or flight

and so Pharaoh made me a leader
a conjured snake
from the staff of his court
realising these plague dreams
that make me
are not nightmares to be fought
but a destiny in prophecy
to be passed on
to be taught
freedom becomes me
but unlike Moses
i won't leave

A POEM ON THE WALL

houseproud in our first flat together
we squabble over our housewarming gift from your dad
a coveted   yet tatty   old world map
nicotine stains adding centuries to its age
now pride of place in our kitchen
and there we are   deep in preparations
plotting courses of where we will go
once we are married
and ideas come to me
like muscle memories to my lips
and before i know it
i am   off the map
deep into how biased towards the northern hemisphere
the relative areas on this Mercator projection actually are
how Africa   and the sub-continent   and South America
have been made   proportionally   smaller
an ego thing   a big swinging ego thing
and how we have all learned   to accept this
and never   challenge it
i mean logically
how do you fit the diversity of Africa's flora and fauna
into a space as small as Europe
we should have noticed this

you smirk knowingly
never disrupting the flow of me

and suddenly i am riffing on the partition of India
speaking passionately about how house masters
have been drawing lines   for centuries
making borderlands of our very souls
splitting families   asunder
in the carving up   of Africa
look there   at the straightness   of these borders
no grounding   or rounding   for natural geological features
and i am heartwarmed and houseproud
just egos   of some white ghosts

and treaties
that had nothing to do with the indigenous peoples
still seen as species
and suddenly i am on to women being disenfranchised
into classifications of race
based on the shapes of a face
and the Holocaust   and Section 28
and how straight white men got so addicted
to drawing lines back then   and conquering
to divide
they are still drawing them now
is that why we called them rulers

but even as i am still pontificating and pointing
to all the lines that should be here and now between us
you erase them all with a kiss made fingertip to lips
recognising the ranting anxiety of this
is me frantically trying to find a beach
even in the twenty-first century
where a black man and a white woman can simply be

fast-forward twelve years
and six years after our separation
and the heirloom is in our heir's room
and i am explaining to him
all about our wedding preparations
how we struggled to find a nation for a honeymoon
that could see Mummy and Daddy as family
and that we didn't owe reparations to
i am explaining to him
how true love can keep such talk
as a passing conversation
had tongue-in-cheek
over washing up together
i am explaining to him
that though some people will always draw lines in sand
love should never have to respect them
and i am heartwarmed and houseproud
over that tatty old map for the first time
as i find he knows it all inherently

HISTORY 101

Maybe i was meant to be
Assimilated offbeat as
Different parts of me
Always
Made more sense in discord
I
Made me in empty classrooms
At the chalkboard
Disruptive influences of memory
A great teacher in these
Manacled and manicured thoughts

(Now read bottom to top)

STOICISM IN STOCKWELL[2]

growing up in London   makes for an intimate relationship
with the law of large numbers
the nature of random
how things are inevitable
even far-off ones
wary of cascade failures of complex systems
but remaining stoic with them
how 1% of a population   being sociopaths
is more than enough   when you live with so many people
how just because *you are never more than ten feet from a rat*
doesn't mean you always see them
or can recognise one

growing up black in London   makes for an intimate
relationship with the law
for in large enough numbers
stop and search stops feeling random
becomes inevitable
and being ever wary   of the failures of this system
makes for antagonisms
but remaining stoic with them
you grow up
seeing the 1% have too much
when you live with so many people
who don't have enough
sometimes you grow up
wanting to tear it all down

2   First Published in The Morning Star - November 2019

DADDY SENSEI

you taught me in war games
in chess
through draughts
on cards
all life's most important lessons
how to lose well
how to win with grace
how to concentrate my effort
how every game
is merely and truly about the player themselves
and their own self-doubt the same

i am hiding in my toy box
i am not six

you taught me in war games
in board games on lazy Sundays
the importance of family
about how arguments should never be allowed to last
how cheating always sours the taste of victory
all life's most important lessons
in sacred hours
on how seeing deeper than your opponent
is a secret weapon
one (when you are good enough at it)
you never have to keep
a secret
a mate in you
checkmate in two

i am in crying in my room
i am not nine

you taught me in war games
the true nature of defeat
that it is not in falling
or flailing

or in failing to rise back to your feet
to meet your enemy again
but actually
in failing to meet yourself again
but once
all life's most important lessons
for me to dine out on
to pass on
to my son

> *i am screaming*
> *it's not fair*
> *slamming doors*
> *i didn't ask to be born*
> *i am not fifteen*

but lately
in all our games
i have found my mind
wandering
found myself in wondering
about our rules of engagement
about what new arrangement of my hand
can trump the cancer card
the Ace of Spades
you now hold
so i fold
let you win again
let you smile again
proud of your student
as we reset the board
one more move
into the game

> *i am explaining*
> *to my son*
> *where you are going*
> *where you have gone*
> *and i feel so young*

MISSIONARY

outside my window
a throng of crows is milling
murmuring loud to baying
a midday bayou mob
that have chased me from sleep
with fires and white cotton hoods

no wait
that is me
still under the duvet

they are puffed chest
in debt-bought best
fronting this Sunday with formal greetings

there proudly being seen
still worshipping the god the white man gave them
while the white man
gave him up

there jealously
still holding the white words on their tongues
like being understood clearly
is enough to be
one of the good ones

next to me
Saturday Night is waking
a face gaunt and haunting
now strangely reminiscent
of Mr Little from history class

and to pass the time
they sang sometimes

he said back then

and *'I've Been Working on the Railroad'*

is still our rhythm…
i replied

…and here endeth the lesson
is Empire-sent
taken as read

i said

and at gravesides
we still sing

Saturday Night asks me
so what are you thinking

nothing much
i reply

assume the position
thinking of England
for at gravesides we still sing

BLOODY BLISTER CHESTERFIELD

sore these eyes
watching a predominantly white audience
and predominantly white panel
discussing the betrayal
of the Windrush generation
and their children
on late night television
via the BBC's (and therefore the UK's)
de facto flagship political show

sore these eyes
red raw reminded
of all those times
that i was the only black man in the room
at a flagship British university
at a British book fair
at my British book launch
in inner city south London
where i was born
as i finally realise
what it is to really feel these accidents of birth
realise why representation matters
realise why they listed us with dogs
realise what really happens to the robots
when the tokens for the metre run out

sore these eyes
rubbed raw by colourblind whataboutisms
of EU nationals
abhorred by the false equivalencies
of the petty Brexit point scoring
as they shout as people drown
fall down and die
and i wonder
what new dis is this
disengaged   disingenuous
disenfranchised or dismissed

they will of course say later
that the audience was invited already
that the panel was invited already
that a week is a long time in politics
there wasn't enough time
to avoid these bad optics
that make these eyes of mine so sore

but you had seventy years
i'll say
from 1948
and nearly fifty years to the day
from rivers of blood
i'll say
how much time do you need
to get better representation
on the nation's flagship politics programme
discussing deportations
misplaced citizenships
and *Go Home* vans
how much time do you need then
for discussing what should be done
about my mum
and my dad
and so many like them
and to do it here
without them

and please   Mr Boomer Man
tell me again
how any of this is a sign
of political correctness gone mad

tell me again
i dare you

REPARATIONS

fuck white privilege!
a friend said
i have   thanks
i said
and here's how it went

of course there was an Oxbridge reject
who bade me beg
who made me sext
persuaded me upon their messages
to keep the sound up
long enough
that they could train me
a Pavlov dog
to pings   like ringing bells
swooshing swipe
to swell

and then of course
there was Range Rover Miss
all horsey jolly hockey sticks
who loved to fly
while being non-stop
as well as on top
and the mental gymnastics
of her riding crop
yes miss   no miss   Fleabag is cool miss…

and then there was
humanitarian of Tinder
(or was it Grindr)
with those photos outside his hut
in deep Uganda
so deep it ran   his saviour brand
Pygmalion to make me
to speak all proper
even in the poetry he made me offer
like he was a deity

and i was his property
this bijou fixer-upper
and *fuck white privilege!*
he once said
i will   thanks
i said
because this is how it went

with once upon a childhood friend
making me a frame of reference
played measure for measure then
grabbing me by the crotch
for the notch in her nook
now quoting EDL conspiracies daily
over on Facebook
her Islamophobia
from page one of the Kristallnacht playbook
and me realising
i was her single-use plastic
the used dildo
she now sells on Craigslist

but before all this
the English teacher obsessed with poetry
when i was seventeen
who took my virginity
and has me still wondering
over a quarter of a century
if they groomed me
played me like Eurydice
had me follow them silently into poetry
so white privilege might eventually
learn to love me
and let me breathe

so yes indeed
i have fucked white privilege
and now i think i'd rather smash the patriarchy
that sold me into this slavery

EXTRA CREDIT

the weather has turned so she has offered him
a lift home   but in three hours of sitting
they haven't moved   though everything has shifted
the sun has set   silence has fallen
and becomes them   uncomfortable
as after a confession   but before absolution

and suddenly   there is nothing
but the deluge   the beating of rain
on the roof   the occasional flash
of angels taking pictures   for posterity
a rumble   of indelible memories
settling into PTSD   grey   a veil of tears
the purr of idling   a chaos engine
tumbling

the weather is glowering
and the pathetic fallacy is there for them to see
a lesson in irony this   they are about to lose
this is too close this is taboo
and the pools gathering in the car park around them
are forming   an inescapable Rubicon

this the start of a story   that will end in betrayal
the heavens have opened   and the spine of tale
is broken

AFTER SOJOURNER TRUTH

going Greek island
hopping one summer
Lesbos was poetry
Hydra a bit heady
Rhodes was colossal
still finding my way
to Ithaca

VOLCANOLOGY

your house had a scent to it
and at five years high
not tall enough to see the mantle
i thought it was volcanoes and lava
i was obsessed by such
and your living room carpet
had the look of it
the hot stuff
and the footstool was the safe bit
and we played this
and you knew stuff
about lava
such grown-up stuff
that i am telling
my own son now
about sulphur and fire toxins
and that smell
so familiar
that i found out later
was the cigarettes
you used to sneak
before we came round

the last time we saw each other
didn't really happen
i saw you   Godmother
but you couldn't see me
still wanting to play
hidden behind the curtains
of your cataracts
in occluded memories
vascular dementia
Dad said

i found out later
that was the cigarettes too
and light one in tribute

OUROBOROS

these snakes
    sell low-hanging apple pie dreams
        all sticky cream and sweet
            that sickly slip and trip
                and catch in the throat so
                    ticky-tacky flaky stodge sewn
                        to dislodge the worthy
                            lump of sinful originality
                                guilty conditioning
                                    all too human…
                                        these snakes
                                            sell empty-headed consumption
                                        the commoditised self
                                    the ever-fresh flesh
                                reaffirmed and peddle pressed
                            treadmill mangled
                        a spinning class of hamster wheels
                    to be wrinkle-free
                bleached and perky
            plumped and succulent breast
cut and stuffed and nipped and tucked
and narcissus plucked
    and stuck
        with spice and sugar
            to eat themselves
                in from their tales
                    and fail to see
                        the endless circular irony
                            in this self-referential
                                self-reverential
                                    inherent inherited incest
                                    the true beauty of beauty as
                                industry
                                and the hell this entails
                            in repetition
                        chasing their fails
                    in repetition

they sell their oil
these snakes
they sell their oil
selling possessions
as less than demonic
all silver-tongued siren song
from forked pitched cacophony
to be legion
for we are many
possessions in prepossession of possessions
these poisoned apple pie dreams
lulling us to sleep
with whispers
eat me, eat me, eat me
these snakes coil
and strike
with shock and awe
selling panaceas
there is no sickness for
they sell their oil
these spoils of war
to grease squeaky wheels
and keep them
poor

FAULT LINE

and i wonder
how many of my white friends
cite me
in THOSE conversations
in their but I have black friends defence
in THOSE conversations
and i wonder how many of them
have passed me in the street
without seeing me
as he just did
conditioned to not see black faces at rush hour
and this thought in repetition
in those weeks when the phone doesn't ring
this thought in repetition
on lonely mornings on the ward
rumbling
threatening the newly built Jenga towers
of talk therapy with restless legs
with lack of sleep   with side effects
with tremor after tremor
tictic   tic

she asks me how i manage being
so extroverted with this

her stabilising hand is cheating the system
she is not a friend
but at least she sees me
SEES me
sees me regularly
dispassionately reassures
restores foundations
tick   tick   tick

for at this hour
self-doubt like me
has a time and a place to be

(A)DRIFT

my truant goddess
i am still where you left me
unfinished and directionless   epic travail
this abandoned ship
you passed   one night   seductively

a thousand thoughts   now set to sea   in pursuit of beauty
without a sure to steer by   or star by which to sail
my truant goddess
i am still where you left me

so cut adrift on twilight's seamless   stardust seas
betrayed by arts   and here be dragons tales
this abandoned ship
you passed   one night   seductively

and stooped to kiss   upon this oft-turned cheek
to stun with bliss   and hold me here   and there
to flail
my truant goddess
i am still where you left me
hanging on the world's edge   on the cusp of Damocles
tenterhooked   and hung against the heavens railed
this abandoned ship
you passed   one night   seductively
to leave me
lost
a last forgotten devotee
to leave me
caught
in jaws of purest whitest wail
my truant goddess
i am still where you left me
this abandoned ship
you passed   one night   seductively
(without the gift of endings)

SOLILOQUY

if it helps
imagine that he is there waiting for you
narrating these unscripted words
to stand to attention
in attack posture
he once learned in a soapbox opera
broadcast service
in Sunday proudflesh on the South Bank
anonymous stopped
imagine that he is baroque tableau
facing the crowds with masterstrokes
archiving the contorted swarming
of an embattled Waterloo

if it helps
imagine that he is there playing
purple puce poetry on pan flutes
sailing burnished barges between garbage scowls
and howls of derision
that he is longing for you
and your laughter
longing for not just desserts
but forever afters
a small acknowledgement
in cold light
of this spot
that someone is out there

if it helps
imagine that he is Nephilim
waiting on his wings
for a cue to stop crying
in the shadows behind the certain
the straw man dying
imagine how his words might read
in a halo of applause
that his testimonies are perfect

65

eidetic recitations of formulas for key lime pie
for space-time rendered slice by slice
a time and place
for honesty breathing excitedly
tender gaps in nature
we all need

if it helps
imagine that he is the sage of Pompeii
listening to the bowels of toppling dominoes
in the skin of pilloried smoke
hearing profound rounds in the squall
with each breath he takes
a lecture note
in our soapbox opera
a pregnant pause
waiting for the dammed dawn to break
and the pennies to drop
anywhere

if it helps
imagine that he is a dog
because you know we treat those better

G

June moon is juju   dancing lights in the passage
a shimmer   in doorways is midsummer
and in your bed in the basement room
we are spent   flushed in afterglowing
and still cooling   a locked security gate
our only thought to modesty   that lingers
as whispers   still dripping   with seething garden promises
slip between the bars   soused in scent markers
pheromones sneering   eye toothed and stealthy
a canine figure   a slinky shadow
fused into copper   stalking a sexstink in iron
and overwrought skin intoxicant   that pollutes
nascent dreaming   as suggestive in my waking
the apparition is rendered flesh and fleeing footsteps

in the morning over breakfast
i tell you all about the visitation
confessing the wet churning of bestial breath upon my neck
you meet the testimony with a look of disbelief
not quite hiding the sharpness of your teeth

420 ARSON

police resources are stretched
and on this day it was unseasonably hot
the sort that one set
and the jet set
were protesting about
and yellow-vested populist
wanted nativist
wanted Brexit
it is late
it is late
and now they
are spoiling for a fight
and just spoiling

away from it all
in the royal park
we spark
police resources too stretched
to catch this real seat of revolution
all kisses should burn like this

PIGEONHOLES

in a world defined
increasingly by identity
i find i have become somewhat
problematic

the first time i realised this
was on the census form
the year that Jedi should have been recognised
as a new religion
despite being founded
a long long time ago
in a galaxy far far away
it is symptomatic
of the clear bright lines
people need to draw
to count those who count
to make divisions arbitrarily
in sexuality
in race
in gender
that belie the continuities of reality
because so many of these
run through the heart of me

because always there in front of me
are boxes
discrete and indiscreet
in neat little columns
with never space for a fifth
discord or diminished
outlined in black
to be marked with a tick
or freed slave X
choose your tribe in *black or blue ink*
so bruising
that *black or blue ink*
(only some colours count   you see)

for i know that some time ago
i would have been *creole* or *mulatto*
derogatory definitions but at least encompassing
now facing being made dull
being rendered flat
being devoid of genetic tricks
freed of muscle memory songs
and melanin's mottled mischief
now *black and white mixed*
as a minstrel am i
other   *please specify*
is black African
is black Caribbean
is black other
other   please specify
and NO you can't tick them all
pick a side to be
pick a side to deny
so every time since
the other box winks
knows it will have my allegiance
as a jack of all shades
master of one

LENSING

at the heart of every black hole
a singularity
infinitely small
infinitesimally deep
intensity affected density
drawing everything into it
an inescapable gravity
and all we see
its event horizon
space-time warping
a phenomenon called *lensing*
swallowing and bending even light
and everything and everything
and everything beyond the horizon
beyond the sight of imaginations
the reach of our eyes
made invisible
as it dies

Andy was a science teacher
now sells cheap lighters to pissed-up punters
to make eighteen pounds for a shelter
the kind that blow up in your pocket   he laughs
says something pithy about *graft*
see me after class
he can't see well without his glasses
but they stopped being a priority
soon after his son died
Andy knows the warping of space-time
knows the atomic weight of misery
knows it practically beyond the theory
how entropy effects empathy
how class war has casualties
truth always the first
cities always warzones
every fight has its purse
Andy warns about unexploded weapons

discarded in doorways
claymores   these human shields
strewn by the side of the road
damaged and stripped of all collateral
eighteen-pound shelters
cannot save you from bombs still falling
but they give you hope
and hope is the killer
Andy is still a teacher

somewhere on the city streets
a singularity
intensity affected density
drawing everything into it
an inescapable gravity
streets will catch
anyone who falls through cracks
dragging them down deep
past the event horizon
through the phenomenon called lensing
beyond the sight of imaginations
and the reach of most eyes
to be crushed and smashed
made invisible
as they die

CLARET

6 am on a Sunday
and at this hour
even the whitest parts of the city
are coloured
the vigil lamppost is brown
and wilted flowers
petal form rusty puddles
red wax harder to shift than blood
gravitational rings
cling to flagstones
halo debris for heavenly bodies
in monument hallmark monoliths
shrine after shrine
without an icon or a god
time after time
settling
always settling

and writ large across this scene
how passive aggression is a luxury
like everything else
how lives cost more in certain postcodes
how sleep itself can be a luxury
let alone a bed
as a free sheet newspaper
rolls like tumbleweed
past the servant class spoor
Quixote windmills
with some heavy millstone headline
about youths being feral
leaving its mark everywhere
it lies
it lies
through the echoes still spilling
from the railway arch bar
in resonant chorus plinking star bright
splashing tin soundscapes

so many freshly polished surfaces
for newly polished accents
this is white noise
alien to this space
yet all encompassing
the waters we swim in

6am on a Sunday
and the colours are running
where the gutters are porous
and awash with darker blood
full-bodied and complex
melanin like tannins
metallic and sharp on the palette
painting the scene

talking about politics is a luxury
the blue lights are singing
in familiar songs from the Odyssey
and passive aggression is a luxury
and like everything else
lives cost more in certain postcodes
the blue lights are singing

it is 6am on a Sunday
and at this hour
the danger is in believing
everything they always said about you
the danger is in believing
the words given freely
at this hour
and at every hour
the danger is in believing
the whitest parts of the city
are only ever coloured by their history
and missing
the red in this morning
that you are finally awake for

NET GAINS

the fisherman went out 'til eight
to catch the fish
to adorn his plate
the fisherman went out 'til nine
to catch the fish
to buy more lines
the fisherman went out 'til ten
to catch the fish
to pay more men
the fisherman went out 'til twelve
to catch the fish
and some more to sell
for this is progress and the beast loves progress
the fisherman went out before dawn
to the secret place where fishes spawned
to catch the fish
to buy boats and more
nets and canners and an office and halls
and papers and pens and desks with drawers
and the fisherman's boats went out all day
to catch the fish
to his company pay
until the need
for him to fish had gone away
for this is progress
and the beast loves progress

until sitting at his desk
on the dock on the bay
with spreadsheets and meetings
and accountants to pay
the fisherman dreamt of the simpler days
that had finished at the stroke of eight
when the only catch
was for his plate
and his only wish
was chips

UBUNTU

we are all intrinsically socialist
within our own self-identified tribe
it is all about who you are
are prepared to call family
and to recognise

and we called the sundowning
orange clouds

confide

she lost me in the orange clouds today

i am
because we are
to each
according to our need

FATHERLAND

in our last World Cup together
this is what you taught me

how a game means so much more
with something riding on it
how people who wager merely money
are all small stakes gamblers
how it is better to wager dreams
this is what you taught me

in our last World Cup together
you lamented all you'd never see
in the fallibility and fragility of your being
the inevitability of your failure
the inevitability of penalties
as i lamented all you'd never see
and how biased the heavens
and how mortal referees
this is what you taught me
along with something mumbled about Nietzsche
in the seizure that is grief
Thus Spoke Zarathustra
how the hand of god is a cheat
as is every deus ex machina
how it makes all stories weak
in our last World Cup together
something mumbled about Nietzsche
about what doesn't kill you
something mumbled about stronger
as i had ever needed to be
such
this is what you taught me
better to wager these dreams
money is for the small stakes gamblers
we have family
and did i ever call you *daddy*
i wonder

about my memories
i wonder how i've sepiaed these
England lost to Croatia
having taken the lead
how this was always our country
this is what you taught me
in the seizure that is grief

how a game means so much more
with something riding on it
especially when that is more
than all it seems
how keeping score is all about memories
and how we sepia these
how keeping score is all about memories
and how our history
is identity
this is what you taught me
in our last World Cup together
as you begged me to believe
to believe in all the places
you were going
or thought you were
in suburbia
in the 1970s
how people who wager merely money
are all small stakes gamblers
how it is better
to wager your dreams
and win family
and as you bet your life
you finally win at family
it is our last World Cup together
and in suburbia
you dream
and as i read ahead
to final day
i wonder
what might have been

ACKNOWLEDGEMENTS

Special thanks to Rodney and Ann Dove (my ever-patient parents), and Susan Newton and Serena Malcolm (my wonderful sisters), who together formed the loving family that made growing up a bit different, more fun than frightening.

Thank you to my son Rufus Hamblyn Dove, who has been an unceasing inspiration and motivation throughout this process. Thanks also to his wonderful mum Laura Hamblyn, and her mum Elizabeth Payne, for raising a young man that we can all be proud of, even when he is generating challenging theories, which have seeded many of the pieces in this collection.

There isn't the space for the amount of love I have for the Boomerang Club team right now, for all their support, all the advice, and for creating a safe space for free expression, that allows for the full spectrum of human experience. Jake Wild Hall, Joel Auterson, Tyrone Lewis, Antonia Jade King, Peter DeGraft-Johnson, and Caroline (Mama Caz) Moy have been instrumental.

The teams at Once Upon a Mic and Genesis Slam, that complete my triangle of 'home' events in London, Horacio Toulouse la Maga, Jah-Mir Early and Math Jones, and Sara Hirsch, Caroline Teague and Dan Simpson: thanks, folks.

Big love to Peter Hayhoe at Muddy Feet Poetry for producing some priceless videos of some of the pieces in this book.

And all the wonderful colleagues and supporters from the London poetry scene and beyond (in alphabetical order for the sake of maintaining friendships): Amy Acre, Huw Bevan, Hannah Chutzpah, GB Clarkson, Rebecca Cooney, Sadie Davison, Laurie Eaves, Tessa Foley, Maya Fraser, Natasha Gilbert, Carys Hannah, Robin Lamboll, Steve Larkin, Carmina Masoliver, Barbara O'Donnell, Gboyega Odubanjo, Hannah Raymond-Cox, Fay Roberts, Myriam San Marco, Daisy Thurston-Gent, and Alexander Woodward.

The seriously magical thing about poetry is that it has some of the best people, and some of its serious talents also provide amazing advice and support to us newbies on the way through… if I have seen far… shoulders of giants… some of the giants I am grateful to: Raymond Antrobus, Anthony Anaxagorou, Kat

Francois, Glyn Maxwell, Roger Robinson, and Joelle Taylor.

And last, but by no means least, massive thanks to Sumaya Kilani for the simply gorgeous cover design, and to Clive Birnie and Bridget Hart for belief in my words that made this whole collection possible.

Excelsior![3]

---

3 Acknowledgements are the last thing you actually write on a book, I think, so this is the just-finished moment, right HERE.